W9-CTL-118

First published in Switzerland under the title *Danke, kleiner Apfel!*

First published in the United States, Great Britain, Canada,
Australia, and New Zealand in 2001 by North-South Books,
an imprint of Nord-Süd Verlag AG, Gossau Zürich, Switzerland.
First paperback edition published in 2003 by North-South Books.
Distributed in the United States by North-South Books Inc., New York.

Library of Congress has cataloged an earlier edition. LC# 2001269281

ISBN 0-7358-1426-0 (trade edition)
10 9 8 7 6 5 4 3 2
ISBN 0-7358-1427-9 (library edition)
10 9 8 7 6 5 4 3 2
ISBN 0-7358-1781-2 (paperback edition)
10 9 8 7 6 5 4 3 2 1
Printed in Belgium

For more information about our books,
and the authors and artists who create them,
visit our web site: www.northsouth.com

A Michael Neugebauer Book
NORTH-SOUTH BOOKS / NEW YORK / LONDON

Little Apple

A Book of Thanks

Brigitte Weninger

Anne Möller

Look at this little apple.
It is so round and smooth and pretty.

Some apples are red, others yellow or green
—and some are all three!

Apples are sweet, juicy, and very good for you.
Even the birds know that!

If you cut open an apple,
you will discover a secret:
There's a little star
hidden inside!

In this little star are the brown apple pips.

If you plant one of the little pips in damp earth, it wakes up. It swells and bulges, then takes root and a shoot grows out of it.

In a few years the little shoot becomes a beautiful apple tree.

In spring the tree is covered with
delicate pinkish-white apple blossoms.
Many bees come to sip the blossoms' nectar.
As they do, they carry pollen from
blossom to blossom.

In summer the blossoms turn into ovaries.
Every day they grow a little bigger and rounder.

Rich earth and warm rain help them to grow,
and the warm sun makes them sweet and juicy.
By autumn they are delicious ripe apples.

The farmer picks them from the tree.

And then I have an apple to eat.
I hope that other children have healthy fruit to eat, too.
I am so thankful for this little apple.